Contents

Together forever, eternally

In July 2009 David and Victoria Beckham celebrated their tenth wedding anniversary. To mark the occasion Victoria had a new tattoo on the inside of her left wrist. The Hebrew words of the tattoo mean 'Together forever, eternally'. David had a ring of ten roses, a rose for each year they have been together, tattooed on his left arm.

WOW!

For their thirteenth wedding anniversary it is rumoured that David made a book full of the couples' memories, which charted their love story.

"I know a lot of things have been said about us being too young and not married, and being bad role models for young people. But we love each other, we're best friends and we're ready to be parents. I think that's a good example to set."

In 2008 David also arranged a secret ceremony to renew their wedding vows. A few close friends and family gathered at their home 'Beckingham Palace' in Hertfordshire. Victoria only found out what was happening on the day. The quiet celebration was a far cry from their glitzy wedding nine years before.

David and Victoria's wedding was a media sensation. The love story of a pop princess and a football hero was always in the news. Within a few years of meeting they had a baby.

Some people criticised them for not being married. But, David and Victoria had big plans for their wedding day. The first hint that something special was being planned was the invitations bearing their own crest. The marriage took place on 4 July 1999 at Luttrellstown Castle in Ireland. The 'celebrity royals' sat on golden thrones and the bride wore a crown. Interest in the wedding reached fever pitch because the couple made an exclusive wedding photo deal with *OK!* magazine.

David and Victoria in September 2009. The occasion was the launch of the David Beckham range for Adidas.

TOP TIP

"If you love someone, you want to treat them, surprise them, remind them how you feel, whether that means a weekend away somewhere, or a bowl of fruit in the morning laid out in the shape of a heart. I know Victoria thinks I'm romantic like that." David

Meet the families

David claims that on their first date he knew he'd marry Victoria one day. The couple admit their relationship works because they like being at home together with their children. Family life is important to both of them and both of them come from close families.

WOW!

Victoria's father Tony was the lead singer of a few bands in the 1960s. He played the Lyceum in London with his band the Soniks. The Soniks still gets together for charity events.

Victoria is still close to mother Jackie and father Tony. He arranges security and transport for the Beckhams.

Victoria Caroline Adams was born on 17 April 1974 in Harlow, Essex. Her parents are businessman Anthony Adams and Jacqueline Adams. When Victoria was three the family moved to Goffs Oak, Hertfordshire. They bought a large house where Anthony did lots of the building work himself. Anthony also started a successful business as an electrical wholesaler. He could afford to give Victoria, her younger sister Louise and brother Christian a comfortable lifestyle. One of Anthony's prized possessions was a brown second-hand Rolls Royce. Victoria hated it because she was teased about it at school. She yearned for an ordinary car like the other kids.

INSPIRATION

David says his father Ted is his inspiration: "The training he gave me as a kid has got me to where I am today... "

Money was always tight for the Beckhams. David 'Ted' Beckham did all kinds of jobs to support his family. His main job was a gas fitter but sometimes he did two jobs at a time. His wife Sandra worked as a hairdresser. David was born on 2 May 1975 in Leytonstone, London. He has two sisters Lynne and Joanne. The Beckhams had a small house and garden with a park next door. This was all that David needed as he'd inherited his father's love of football.

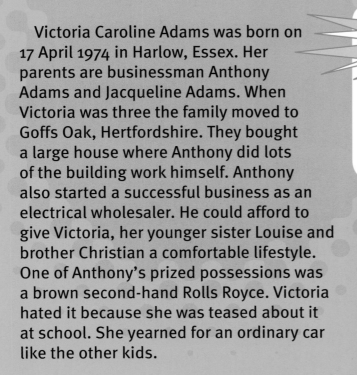

David's father Ted and his mother Sandra. Ted works as a gas fitter and the family live in Essex.

Childhood

Victoria always felt she didn't fit in with the other school kids. At Goffs Oak Primary School she remembers dancing by herself in the playground. In the classroom her teacher destroyed her self-confidence. Things didn't improve at St Mary's secondary school. Her immaculate school uniform made her stand out from the other pupils. Victoria claims that being an 'ugly duckling with spots' didn't help either. Luckily, she really enjoyed her dance classes after school and did well in them.

TOP TIP

"If I am teaching kids, the most important thing I try to get across is to enjoy the game and enjoy learning skills. That was the great thing about playing with my dad. We would work on passing, crossing and shooting for hours and hours." David

Victoria's class teacher at infant school said: "It's a pity they don't have a **remedial** class here Victoria, because that's where you belong." Victoria is on the top row in the middle of this photo.

David was popular at school but football was his first love. He practised every day after school and at the weekends. Like his dad Ted he was an avid Manchester United supporter. For Christmas all he wanted was a new Manchester United strip.

Aged eight David joined the Ridgeway Rovers of the Enfield District League. At eleven he came top at the Bobby Charlton's Soccer Skills Tournament. It was obvious that the young Beckham had talent but he was small for his age. At thirteen it came as quite a blow when his teacher told him: "You'll never play for England, because you're too small and not strong enough."

INSPIRATION

Victoria loves all the old musicals and as a girl her dream was to star in a West End musical. *Fame* was her favourite musical and in those days Barry Manilow was one of her favourite singers!

David's school report in 1987 said: "David has ability but he finds it difficult to concentrate on his work. His tendency to chat and giggle in class has seriously **impeded** his progress."

High kicks and kick offs

Victoria tried hard at school but she wasn't **academic**. Dancing and singing were in her blood. She dreamed of going to stage school but her parents were against it. Instead she stuck out school and left with five GCSEs. At seventeen, she enrolled on a three-year course at Laine's, a theatre arts college in Surrey.

TOP TIP

"Message to the underdog: I am the most successful person who has ever come out of Laine's. It doesn't matter what you look like, it's all about hard work, determination and **self-belief**."
Victoria

During Victoria's school years, every night of the week was spent at a dance class or a rehearsal.

Victoria admits she's not the best dancer in the world but says that she's always worked hard at it. In the final year at Laine's she was in the back row of the chorus for the end-of-year show. Nevertheless, Victoria gave it all she'd got. After college Victoria got her first professional part in a touring musical called *Bertie*.

Meanwhile, David was perfecting his skills on the pitch. He played for local teams but soon professional clubs were beginning to take an interest. **Talent scouts** from Manchester United were on to him by the time he was eleven. On 2 May 1989, David's 14th birthday, he had a meeting with Alex Ferguson. The Manchester United manager offered him a six-year contract with the club.

At sixteen David kicked off as a youth trainee for Manchester United. This meant being away from home but David settled into his new life in Manchester quickly. In October 1992, aged just seventeen, he made his **debut** for the Manchester United first team.

David, aged ten, with local team Ridgeway Rovers. David is in the front row, first left.

Spice up your life

' *WANTED RU 18–23 with the ability to sing/dance? RU streetwise, outgoing, ambitious, dedicated?*' In early 1994, this small advert in *The Stage* newspaper caught Victoria's eye. She answered the advert and was auditioned by father and son management team, Bob and Chris Herbert. At the time, boy bands such as Take That and East 17 dominated the pop scene.

The Herberts were looking to form a girl band. Five girls, including Victoria, were picked from auditions around the country. The girls moved in together and began working on songs and dance routines. After a few changes in the line-up the final members of the band included Victoria Adams, Geri Halliwell, Melanie Brown, Melanie Chisholm and Emma Bunton. In March 1995 they signed a contract with manager Simon Fuller. Soon afterwards there was a record deal with Virgin.

In 1997, the band met Prince Charles. Victoria has said, "Right from the beginning I said I wanted to be as famous as Persil Automatic." By now the Spice Girls were famous all over the world.

In June 1996 the Spice Girls finally released their first single, *Wannabe*. The world was about to discover 'girl power'!

Wannabe went to number one in the UK and in 30 other countries. 'Spicemania' hit America the following year. The Spice Girls became the most popular British band to conquer America since the Beatles. They also became known as Scary, Baby, Ginger, Sporty and Posh Spice.

HONOURS BOARD

Spice Girls UK number one singles include:

Wannabe (1996)
Say You'll Be There (1996)
2 Become I (1996)
Who Do You Think You Are? (1997)
Spice Up Your Life (1997)
Too Much (1997)
Viva Forever (1998)
Goodbye (1998)
Holler / Let Love Lead the Way (2000)

Victoria, the teenage ugly duckling, was called Posh because of her sleek hair and polished looks. She caught the eye of many fans, including the up and coming midfielder for Manchester United, David Beckham. He first saw Victoria in the Spice Girls video *Say You'll Be There*. He asked his sister Joanne to find out more about the glamorous Spice Girl …

The Spice Girls are the most successful girl band of all time. Almost overnight the girls became world famous.

Posh and Becks

When David and Victoria met for the first time he was the shy right-winger for Manchester United with little time for girls. She was a super famous singer for one of the top bands in the world. She also had a boyfriend. None of this mattered and they soon fell in love. David said at the time: "I like Victoria for herself ... I'd like her if she worked in Tesco."

INSPIRATION

"I know I would sacrifice anything for my boys (David and sons), including my career, even though I also know that they would never ask me to."
Victoria

In 1999 the Beckhams bought Rowneybury House in Hertfordshire. The newspapers nicknamed the large country house 'Beckingham Palace', a play on the real royal residence Buckingham Palace.

In the early days they had to keep their relationship secret. Their first date was at a small Chinese restaurant in Chingford. The place was so unfashionable that nobody recognised them. Their first kiss was in a car park in the east end of London. At the time, Victoria was often jetting off abroad touring or promoting the band. David was one of the rising new stars at Manchester United. During the football season he was training and playing football all week. It was difficult for them to meet up but they kept in touch on the phone every day.

David suffers from Obsessive-Compulsive Disorder (OCD). This means he is very tidy. At home all his belongings have to be placed in neat rows. And, he has a new pair of football boots for each match.

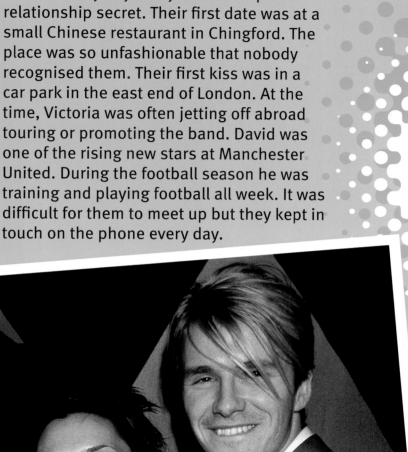

News of David and Victoria's romance soon leaked to the press. Stories about them were everywhere. First of all Victoria moved into David's penthouse in Cheshire. Then, during the Spice Girls World Tour in 1998, Victoria became pregnant. Brooklyn Joseph Beckham was born in March 1999. Four months later David and Victoria were married in Ireland.

Pregnant Posh and beaming Beckham. The young couple always looked happy and in love.

A day in the life of the Beckhams

After 11 number one singles and a smash-hit film, *Spice World* (1997), the Spice Girls split in 2000. That year, Victoria made her first **documentary** for television called *Victoria's Secrets*. In 2001 she wrote her **autobiography** *Learning to Fly* and started her solo music career. In 2002 the Beckhams had their second child, Romeo and Victoria filmed her second documentary, *Being Victoria Beckham*.

TOP TIP

"Preseason is where you get the stability for the rest of the season. I'll never perform at my highest level unless I'm 100 per cent fit. That's one of my biggest **attributes**, the energy I've got on the field. For me, training is as important as the games." David

Victoria promoting her autobiography.

Life as a Spice Girl could be stressful and exhausting. These days Victoria is in charge of her professional life, which includes her own fashion line. She fits work around the important business of being a mother. In many ways she's like any mum. She does the school run and she plays football in the garden. However, she's also a self-confessed workaholic who thrives on the drive and determination it takes to succeed.

David has always trained hard. He is probably the most famous sports person in the world but his working day is the same as any other footballer's. During the football season he must stick to a strict training routine. David claims that his routine hasn't changed much over the years but these days he's more focused: "I used to practice thirty free kicks a day. As I've gotten older, I've learned that less is more. I'll take 10 free kicks a day and make sure those 10 are focused." Like all footballers he cannot drink, take drugs or do any dangerous sports.

These days, David is more confident in public. As England Captain he was a strong leader.

The football legend

As a boy David dreamed of playing for Manchester United. And, for many years it was a dream job. In 1996 he wowed the crowd by scoring against Wimbledon from the halfway line. He went on to become famous for scoring from free kicks. By twisting his foot when he kicked the ball he made fantastic shots at goal. The accuracy of his passing also set up many goals.

INSPIRATION

The Beckhams are a winning team. When the going gets tough they support each other. Victoria was there to help David through the traumatic 1998 World Cup in which David was sent off. He was her rock when kidnappers threatened to snatch Victoria and baby Brooklyn in 2000.

David was 21 when he played for England for the first time.

"I don't worry about any other players ... I've always concentrated on what my job is more than anything, more than how good the other team is, no matter who the opponent is – even off the field."
David

When David met Victoria he was a football hero, but in the next few years he raised his game. In the 1998–1999 season Manchester United won the Treble (the Premier League, FA Cup and UEFA Champions League). They went on to win the league in 2000, 2001 and 2002. David enjoyed these years but the relationship between him and manager Alex Ferguson had started to sour. Ferguson believed that David's life as a celebrity wasn't good for his football career.

David made his debut for England in 1996. He was a star player in the qualifying matches for the 1998 FIFA World Cup. Unfortunately, he was sent off in the match against Argentina. Many people blamed him for England losing the match and being knocked out of the World Cup. Some newspapers printed terrible stories about him and many fans turned against him. He even received death threats. It was a difficult time but he drew strength from the experience and in November 2000 David became England Captain.

David dons the Manchester United strip and yet another hairstyle in 2002.

19

Making the right moves

In 2001 David was awarded the BBC Sports Personality of the Year. This was in recognition of his great performance as England Captain. It came shortly after his superb goal against Greece in the final qualifying match for the 2002 FIFA World Cup. The winning shot curled through the air before firing into the net. The fans were getting behind him again and and the **media** was back on David's side. He captained the England squad at the 2002 World Cup in Japan. Unfortunately, the team only made it to the quarter-finals.

At Real Madrid David played with great players such as the Brazilian strikers Ronaldo and Robinho.

In June 2003 David finally left Manchester United to join top Spanish club Real Madrid. Fans were sad to see him go but they were not surprised. Stories about the arguments between Alex Ferguson and David had been in the news. Ferguson even cut David's face when he kicked a football boot at him. Playing for Real Madrid was a great opportunity for David but it came at a cost. Victoria and the boys preferred to stay in England. David and Victoria were

WOW!

David and Victoria have three sons called Brooklyn (born 1999), Romeo (born 2002), Cruz (born 2005) and a daughter, Harper (born 2011). They named their first son Brooklyn because they were in Brooklyn, New York, when Victoria became pregnant. Romeo came about because they are a romantic couple. They chose Cruz because they liked their friend Tom Cruise's name. Harper is named after Harper Lee – the author of Victoria's favourite book, *To Kill a Mockingbird*.

often apart and there were rumours and **allegations** in the press that David had an affair in Madrid. Fortunately, the Beckhams were strong enough to get through this difficult time in their marriage.

In November 2003 David went to Buckingham Palace to receive an OBE from the Queen. The award was given for his services to football.

All for a good cause

David Beckham has said: "Surely there is no reward more precious than saving the life of a child? Their futures remain in our hands."

WOW!

In 2009 the Beckham's oldest son Brooklyn made his first charity trip on behalf of Save the Children. Victoria said: "I'm pleased Brooklyn is learning that by helping and joining other children he can play a role in making his generation the greatest yet."

Proceeds from the Full Length and Fabulous Ball went to the NSPPC and the Victoria and David Beckham Trust.

David and Victoria are devoted parents. They also have a special way with other children. They have formed a close relationship with heart patient Kirsty Howard. The young girl has a life-threatening illness but helps raise money to support other ill children. In 2001 Kirsty was the England team mascot. David held her hand as they walked onto the pitch at Old Trafford. Over the years, David has met and contacted many ill children. He knows that a call from him can give a child a huge lift and help them get better.

The Beckhams help many children's charities and have set up the Victoria and David Beckham Trust. One of their favourite charities is the NSPCC (National Society for the Prevention of Cruelty to Children). In 2002 they raised over £300,000 for the NSPCC when they hosted a lavish World Cup party. In 2006 they held a glitzy pre-world cup party at Beckingham Palace called the Full Length and Fabulous Ball. The guest list included Kate Moss and P Diddy. Gordon Ramsay cooked a feast in the kitchen and Robbie Williams and James Brown entertained the crowd.

In 2002 Kirsty and David presented the Jubilee Baton to the Queen during the opening ceremony for the Commonwealth Games.

California Dreaming

David was England captain throughout the 2006 FIFA World Cup. During the tournament he became the first English player to score a goal in three different World Cups. Unfortunately, England was knocked out of the cup in the quarter-final against Portugal. The next day David stepped down as captain and for a while he was out of the England squad. Meanwhile David was in **negotiations** with Major League Soccer club Los Angeles Galaxy.

WOW!

In May 2008 David thrilled Galaxy fans when he popped in a goal from 70 yards out. The goal against Kansas City Wizards was his second for Galaxy. It was also the second time that David had scored a goal from his team's half of the pitch.

The Beckhams often attend glamorous events in California, such as the Oscars.

In January 2007 David signed a record-breaking contract with the Californian club making him the highest paid player in Major League Soccer. In June 2007 David played his last matches for Real Madrid. He ended his time at the club on a high with Real scooping the La Liga (the league) title for the first time since he'd joined them. The next month David kicked off his new career in America.

In 2007 the Beckhams were rarely out of the news. First there was their much-hyped move to LA! Many people were excited about the arrival of the glamorous couple. Football fans hoped that David's fame would make the sport more popular in America. The actor Tom Cruise promised to hold a party to introduce them to other Hollywood A-list Celebrities. **Paparazzi** followed the Beckhams wherever they went. Victoria added to the drama with the release of another documentary, *Victoria Beckham: Coming to America.*

INSPIRATION

In 2007, Victoria got back together with the *Spice Girls* for her sons Brooklyn, Romeo and Cruz. She wanted her boys to see her as a famous pop star!

At the end of 2007 there was the Spice Girls reunion. The girls embarked on a worldwide tour, performing 47 sell-out shows. The girls brought all their children on the stage.

Fashion, footy and beyond

Victoria's love of clothes has made her one of the most photographed women in the world. In her time she's squeezed into some tight outfits and tottered around on some killer heels. These days she's taking fashion very seriously. Since 2006 she has launched more than four fashion ranges.

David's soccer school provided free places for children who couldn't afford the fees. David is keen to promote women's football and includes girls at the school.

WOW!

David holds the record for the highest number of England caps for an outfield (any player other than the goal keeper) player, this means he has played for England more than any other outfielder ever!

First Victoria set up the designer sunglasses label called DVB (David and Victoria Beckham) Eyewear. Next came a line of denim called DVB Style, followed by his-and-her fragrances called Intimately Beckham. In 2007 Victoria's cosmetic line V-Sculpt was launched in Tokyo, Japan. In 2008 she launched her dress collection, ten dresses inspired by the 1950s. She has scooped awards and received praise from high places for her fashion achievements. David is a style **icon** too.

Over the years he's experimented with many hairstyles and added new tattoos. His wardrobe has included anything from smart suits to torn jeans. He's worn ethnic beads and diamond studs. Some people thought he got it wrong when he wore a sarong but he kick-started a new trend for men.

David enjoys fashion but his major love will always be football. In 2005 he launched the first David Beckham Academy in London. A second academy followed in Los Angeles. In 2012 David expressed interest in buying a Major League Soccer team when his new two-year contract with LA Galaxy ends in 2014. So watch this space...

In 2006 Victoria published a book packed with fashion advice called That Extra Half an Inch: Hair, Heels and Everything In Between.

WOW!

As well as modelling for Roberto Cavalli, Marc Jacobs and Emporio Armani, Victoria has appeared on covers of Vogue and Elle magazines.

The impact of the Beckhams

In the beginning it was the Spice Girl and the Manchester United star player. Quickly, they became known as Posh and Becks. David has become possibly the most famous sports person in the world. Victoria has transformed herself from a music artist to a style icon. This celebrity force has the potential to sell anything from underwear and tickets to a charity ball, to football classes and designer glasses.

TOP TIP

"You have to remember that when you are performing you become a celebrity, but you are not saving lives. It's not that important." Victoria

In LA, the Beckhams are often photographed together. Family life is more important to them than fame, money and success.

David and Victoria are lucky to have made considerable money doing the things they love best. In 2012 the couple amassed £44 million, putting them third on Forbes' 'Highest-paid celebrity couples' list. They are believed to be worth around £165 million, and the future looks bright, too.

In 2012 the Beckhams played important roles at the London 2012 Games. David was part of the successful Olympic bid and Victoria took to the stadium, with her fellow Spice Girls, to perform during the Olympic Closing Ceremony. David also signed a new contract with LA Galaxy that will see the Beckhams stateside for at least the next two years.

With a Spice Girls musical, *Viva Forever*, set to open in the West End, London, in 2012, both Victoria and David will remain in the spotlight for many more years to come.

WOW!

David is the first sports person to appear on the cover of the American magazine Vanity Fair and the first male to appear on the cover of UK magazine Marie Claire.

INSPIRATION

The Beckhams are inspired by children and support many children's charities. In 2005, David became a goodwill ambassador with a focus on the Sports for Development programme for UNICEF. In recent years he has visited Africa and Thailand for the organisation. The plight of suffering children worldwide is a cause close to the Beckhams' hearts.

David and Victoria are probably the most famous couple in the world. They are a winning combination that has become known as Brand Beckham.

Have you got what it takes to be like the Beckhams? Try this!

1) Do you have an outstanding talent?
a) Yes! People are always saying it!
b) I'm good at something and try hard at it.
c) No. I'm good at lots of different things.

2) Do you live, sleep and dream your special talent?
a) I practise any spare moment I have.
b) I try to practise most days.
c) No, I just live, sleep and dream.

3) Have you joined clubs and classes to get better at your chosen talent?
a) Yes, that's how I learn ways of improving.
b) I'm looking into it.
c) I don't like joining clubs or classes.

4) Do you dream of fame and fortune?
a) Yes, I'm determined to be successful.
b) Yes and I'm always thinking of ways to make it happen.
c) Of course! But I know it's only a dream.

5) How do you feel about working or training hard to get what you want?
a) I'll do anything it takes – within reason!
b) I'm not afraid of hard work but I still want a social life and time for me.
c) School work and having fun with my mates takes up all my time.

6) Do you think you could handle the pressure of being constantly in the public eye?
a) Yes! That's just part of being famous.
b) Most of the time but I would get annoyed if the paparazzi tried to photograph really personal moments.
c) No. I would be a nervous wreck!

RESULTS

Mostly As: You're full of confidence and that's a good start for being a success in anything. David has a real talent for football, but Victoria has never claimed to be the best at anything but has always worked hard. So, even if you're mediocre at something perhaps your commitment and determination will help you achieve your goals.

Mostly Bs: You have the potential to be like the Beckhams. Remember it isn't important to be the best at everything. Never lose sight of the fact that you can do things because you enjoy them and not because you want to become rich and famous. Now is the time to start joining clubs and exploring your talents further.

Mostly Cs: You obviously shun the limelight. There's nothing wrong with that. However, perhaps you haven't thought much about your future yet. Now is the time to think about what you want to do. Having a sport or hobby helps you to keep a balance. It's really important to remember that you don't have to be famous to be a success in life!

Glossary

academic   Describes someone who is clever and good at learning.

allegation   A statement that may not be true and may suggest someone has done something wrong or illegal.

attribute   A quality that a person has; a good part of their character.

autobiography   A book about a person's life, written by the person. *Learning to Fly* was written by Victoria Beckham.

debut   Someone's first appearance in a role.

documentary   A television or radio programme that gives real facts and information about a subject or person.

icon   A famous person whose fame usually outlives them. Elvis Presley and Marilyn Monroe are icons.

impeded   To have struggled with problems caused by somebody else or circumstances beyond your control while you are trying to achieve something.

media   A collective term for newspapers, magazines, radio, television and the information on the Internet.

negotiations   The process of discussing something so that an agreement can be reached between two or more groups or people.

paparazzi   Photographers who follow famous people and take their photographs to sell to newspapers and other parts of the media.

remedial   An old-fashioned term used to describe classes to teach people with difficulties in reading and writing.

self-belief   Trust and faith in your own abilities.

talent scouts   People who are always on the look out for people who have outstanding skills or looks, especially for careers in sport, music, dancing, acting and modelling.

Index